365 Creative Writing Prompts

The Fiction Strategies Book

By. t.m.crane

Parthenon Publishing
ISBN: 978-1548249328

Table of Contents

Introduction...1

Chapter One – From Youth to Adulthood...............................4

Chapter Two – Describing Sounds 25

Chapter Three – Murder..34

Chapter Four – Unrequited love...48

Chapter Five – Stories of Friendship.................................... 57

Chapter Six – Learning about Narrative – Stories of People...................... 67

Chapter Seven – Adjectives 79

Chapter Eight – Fantasy 86

Chapter Nine – Erotica... 100

Chapter Ten – Science Fiction 109

Chapter Eleven – Historical Literature 115

Chapter Twelve – Colors..119

Chapter Thirteen – Contemporary Fiction 127

Chapter Fourteen – Love Stories 140

Chapter Fifteen – Plot Scenarios 149

Chapter Sixteen – Mystery 162

Chapter Seventeen – Hope..182

Chapter Eighteen - Sports 193

Chapter Nineteen – Westerns 197

Chapter Twenty – Travel 207

Chapter Twenty One – Action and Adventure.................... 213

Chapter Twenty Two – A twist in the Tale 230

Chapter Twenty Three – Memoirs 244

Chapter Twenty Four – Words and sounds 260

Chapter Twenty-Five – Video Games...................................270

Chapter Twenty Six – Birthday Parties 278

Chapter Twenty Seven – Seasons 303

Chapter Twenty Eight – Character Development....................................312

Conclusion 330

Introduction

The idea of this book is to help potential writers to come up with the most unique ideas that they can when it comes to writing fiction. The prompts contained within this book are sufficient for a new topic every day of the year, and although the story may sometimes seem obvious, that's where the writer needs to step beyond the obvious and come up with stories that use as much imagination as possible, while still keeping within the parameters of the prompt. Some of the prompts that are given in this book may be based upon sounds, either physical sounds or sounds related to the pronunciation of words. There are also prompts that deal with different genres but the writer is asked to step outside of his/her comfort level and think of the scenarios, the backdrop, the characters and the process of going from beginning through to the end. These are all the things you need to imagine in your mind. Remember that the beginning of a story is that part of the story that encourages the reader to go further. The middle of the story is filled with twists and turns and surprise elements that keep the reader glued to the page and the end of the story is what gives a great impact, leaving the reader feeling very glad they read the story.

Fiction writers have been developing and honing their skills since writing was invented! Before that, stories were simply passed down by word of mouth and often formed part of tradition. Make your stories something special by not grasping at the obvious. Thus if the prompt says, "Mary has a new bike and something unexpected awaits her" it doesn't have to be limited to common sense scenarios. Why not let your imagination come up with a story that includes a little mystery? Perhaps the bike will take her toward meeting the man of her dreams. Perhaps she will be in an accident and this will lead to changes in her life.

You will also learn important elements of writing, such as descriptive words or adjectives, as well as learning about how to make your characters talk! Bring characters and objects to life by demonstrating with words who they are. At the end of the day, as long as you keep within the parameters of the prompt, your imagination knows no limits. Introduce drama. Introduce twists and turns in the road. You are asked to work out your story before you start so that you know the direction it will take. One of the best tips I ever had from a story writer was to think up where the story is going. Once you know that, you can create the scenarios that take you there. Step into the world of imagination and allow your fiction to come to life! Your imagination is the only barrier between writing mundane stories and writing stories that will enthrall your readers. The prompts are there to set the seed into the soil. Then the growth of that story is really down to how much you tend the idea and come up with scenarios that are original, fun or exciting to read and that use your imagination. Enjoy it!

www.tmcrane.org/101kids

Chapter One – From Youth to Adulthood

In this exercise, try to imagine the feelings of young adults and put them into perspective in the stories, to make them seem real. Remember, stories don't have to have obvious endings. Twist them and turn them and make the dramas that happen along the way make perfect sense, with added surprise factors.

1)   Mary has turned from child to teen and wants freedom but is she ready?

_____

_____

_____

_____

_____

_____

_____

_____

_____

_____

2)   Elliott is afraid of leaving university and starting up his own business. When he meets Jade, all becomes clear.

_____

_____

_____

_____

_____

_____

_____

_____

3)   Jennifer is having problems persuading her mom that Geoff is worth all the heartache.

_____

_____

_____

_____

_____

_____

_____

_____

_____

_____

_____

_____

_____

_____

4)   Alison wants to go away to college, but her boyfriend is afraid to lose her. Moving on is difficult.

_____

_____

_____

_____

_____

_____

_____

_____

_____

_____

_____

_____

_____

5)   Eleanor is having problems, being forced to look after younger kids in the family, instead of being out having fun like her fellow teens.

_____
_____
_____
_____
_____
_____
_____
_____
_____
_____
_____
_____
_____

6)   Katy has a dilemma. Should she speak up about the advances being made toward her by her employer?

_____
_____
_____
_____
_____
_____
_____
_____
_____
_____
_____
_____

7)   Kayleigh is ashamed of her father's drinking problem and needs to leave home. How will she fare?

_____

_____

_____

_____

_____

_____

_____

_____

_____

_____

_____

_____

_____

_____

8)   Michael has discovered that girls are attracted to him and exploits it big time. However, he never gets past one or two dates.

_____

_____

_____

_____

_____

_____

_____

_____

_____

_____

_____

_____

_____

9)   Veronica is lost and lonely and seeks comfort in Ewan's arms. Will it work?

_____
_____
_____
_____
_____
_____
_____
_____
_____
_____
_____
_____
_____
_____

10)   Kelly has problems with her sexuality and finds it hard to admit that she has feelings for another girl.

_____
_____
_____
_____
_____
_____
_____
_____
_____
_____
_____
_____

11)   Victoria wants to know what will happen when her parents' divorce comes through. Where will life take her?

_____
_____
_____
_____
_____
_____
_____
_____
_____
_____
_____
_____
_____
_____
_____
_____

12)   Emily has trouble learning to keep quiet when it comes to giving friends advice. However, a surprise waits around the corner.

_____
_____
_____
_____
_____
_____
_____
_____
_____
_____
_____
_____
_____
_____
_____
_____

13)   Emile is an artist and wants Wendy to pose naked. Will she?

_____

_____

_____

_____

_____

_____

_____

_____

_____

_____

_____

_____

_____

14)   Paris, France and two students fall in love while on a vacation. Is it Paris or really grown up love?

_____

_____

_____

_____

_____

_____

_____

_____

_____

_____

_____

_____

15)   Kelly finds a bottle on the beach that holds a message, she wishes she had never found.

_____
_____
_____
_____
_____
_____
_____
_____
_____
_____
_____
_____
_____
_____
_____

16)   Roaming the streets after having taken drugs, Kenny has to put the pieces of his life back together again.

_____
_____
_____
_____
_____
_____
_____
_____
_____
_____
_____
_____
_____
_____
_____

17)   Mary's mom died and Mary is left with all of her feelings fighting about the value of life.

_____

_____

_____

_____

_____

_____

_____

_____

_____

_____

_____

_____

_____

_____

_____

18)   Following a move to a new home, Jerry can't seem to get to grips with the local teens until something drastic happens.

_____

_____

_____

_____

_____

_____

_____

_____

_____

_____

_____

_____

_____

19)   Kerry undresses for the first time in front of her boyfriend, but was it worth all of the emotional turmoil?

_____
_____
_____
_____
_____
_____
_____
_____
_____
_____
_____
_____
_____
_____
_____

20)   There are no words left between them. Betray has Melony in its grips.

_____
_____
_____
_____
_____
_____
_____
_____
_____
_____
_____
_____
_____
_____

21)   Katy isn't kidding. Her father is beating her mom and she wants someone to listen – anyone to listen, though no one appears to care.

_____
_____
_____
_____
_____
_____
_____
_____
_____
_____
_____
_____
_____
_____

22)   Petra is unhappy because she is accustomed to getting her own way. Only this time, her father is ready to put his foot down.

_____
_____
_____
_____
_____
_____
_____
_____
_____
_____
_____
_____
_____
_____

23)   Should Elliott Willis get away with what he did to Emily? She thinks not.

_____

_____

_____

_____

_____

_____

_____

_____

_____

_____

_____

_____

_____

_____

_____

_____

24)   The loneliness catches up with Anna as she finds out that her father is being unfaithful to her mother.

_____

_____

_____

_____

_____

_____

_____

_____

_____

_____

_____

_____

_____

_____

_____

_____

25)   Liz wants to trust him. She needs to trust him, but in truth, she can't.

_____
_____
_____
_____
_____
_____
_____
_____
_____
_____
_____
_____
_____

26)   Molly's twin has more luck in life than Molly, though things are about to change.

_____
_____
_____
_____
_____
_____
_____
_____
_____
_____
_____
_____
_____

27)   Leaving home, Laura finds that her new digs are not as tempting as she first thought they would be.

_____

_____

_____

_____

_____

_____

_____

_____

_____

_____

_____

_____

_____

_____

_____

_____

28)   There are no words to describe what Sandra feels when her only child is in a motor cycle accident.

_____

_____

_____

_____

_____

_____

_____

_____

_____

_____

_____

_____

_____

_____

_____

_____

29)   Linda learns that deception isn't the right answer to her dilemma. How will her parents react?

_____
_____
_____
_____
_____
_____
_____
_____
_____
_____
_____
_____
_____
_____
_____

30)   There is no escape. When you owe money, someone's always going to step up and demand it back.

_____
_____
_____
_____
_____
_____
_____
_____
_____
_____
_____
_____
_____

31)   Felicity uses deceit to get what she wants out of Kyle, though he isn't as stupid as she supposes.

_____
_____
_____
_____
_____
_____
_____
_____
_____
_____
_____
_____
_____
_____

32)   The false pregnancy. Will Al fall for it, or will he run in the opposite direction.

_____
_____
_____
_____
_____
_____
_____
_____
_____
_____
_____
_____
_____
_____

33)   Tommy wants to become a champion swimmer, though Elly gives him an ultimatum.

_____
_____
_____
_____
_____
_____
_____
_____
_____
_____
_____
_____
_____
_____

34)   Kelly is found cut and bruised, but dare not explain what really happened.

_____
_____
_____
_____
_____
_____
_____
_____
_____
_____
_____
_____
_____
_____

35)   There's no such thing as luck. It's just the way that your cards are stacked.

_____

_____

_____

_____

_____

_____

_____

_____

_____

_____

_____

_____

_____

_____

_____

_____

_____

36)   Jason hides his alcoholism from his parents, but fate changes his path.

_____

_____

_____

_____

_____

_____

_____

_____

_____

_____

_____

_____

_____

_____

_____

_____

_____

37)   There's a stop light in the road. Phil ignores it and the consequence is fatal.

_____
_____
_____
_____
_____
_____
_____
_____
_____
_____
_____
_____
_____

38)   Stealing a car turns to a nightmare when Jason realizes the significance of what he has done.

_____
_____
_____
_____
_____
_____
_____
_____
_____
_____
_____
_____
_____

39) Mary isn't stupid, but she has been fooled by Hal. Revenge is sweet.

_____

_____

_____

_____

_____

_____

_____

_____

_____

_____

_____

_____

_____

_____

_____

40) Lesley goes on vacation, but gets more than she bargained for.

_____

_____

_____

_____

_____

_____

_____

_____

_____

_____

_____

_____

_____

_____

41)   Mrs. Wallace knows that money is missing from her bank, but how will she confront her son?

_____

_____

_____

_____

_____

_____

_____

_____

_____

_____

_____

_____

_____

_____

_____

42)   Hattie loves being young, free and single, but will Graham change her mind?

_____

_____

_____

_____

_____

_____

_____

_____

_____

_____

_____

_____

Chapter Two – Describing Sounds

In this chapter, you are made aware of sounds. What the writer is to come up with is the atmosphere within a set scenario. For instance, you may be describing the peace and calm of the river or the noise and haste of a crowd during rush hour. Use words wisely and try to come up with words that make the reader hear the noises within the scenario.

43)   The river currents were too strong for Mike to swim against.

_____

_____

_____

_____

_____

_____

_____

_____

_____

_____

_____

_____

_____

_____

_____

_____

_____

_____

_____

_____

_____

_____

_____

_____

44)   The anticipation of the large airport lounge as Pete waits for a plane that will never arrive.

_____
_____
_____
_____
_____
_____
_____
_____
_____
_____
_____
_____
_____
_____
_____
_____
_____
_____
_____
_____
_____
_____
_____
_____
_____
_____
_____
_____
_____
_____

45)   The atmosphere is like ice between Paul and Wendy as the car swerves off the road into the night.

_____

_____

_____

_____

_____

_____

_____

_____

_____

_____

_____

_____

_____

_____

_____

_____

_____

_____

_____

_____

_____

_____

_____

_____

_____

_____

_____

_____

_____

_____

_____

_____

46)   The sounds of Christmas and Molly takes the kids to see the village Christmas tree.

_____
_____
_____
_____
_____
_____
_____
_____
_____
_____
_____
_____
_____
_____
_____
_____
_____
_____
_____
_____
_____
_____
_____
_____
_____
_____
_____
_____
_____
_____
_____
_____
_____
_____
_____
_____
_____

47)   This story is about Ben's journey across the oceans toward a new beginning.

_____

_____

_____

_____

_____

_____

_____

_____

_____

_____

_____

_____

_____

_____

_____

_____

_____

_____

_____

_____

_____

_____

_____

_____

_____

_____

_____

_____

_____

_____

_____

_____

_____

_____

_____

48)   Storms are ruining the crop and Hattie and James have to work hard to save the fruits of their labor.

_____

_____

_____

_____

_____

_____

_____

_____

_____

_____

_____

_____

_____

_____

_____

_____

_____

_____

_____

_____

_____

_____

_____

_____

_____

_____

_____

_____

49)   This story describes the sound of silence in the atmosphere as Patricia says her final farewell to her father.

_____
_____
_____
_____
_____
_____
_____
_____
_____
_____
_____
_____
_____
_____
_____
_____
_____
_____
_____
_____
_____
_____
_____
_____
_____
_____
_____
_____
_____
_____
_____
_____
_____
_____
_____
_____
_____
_____
_____
_____
_____

50)   Thunder and lightning – and the storm brewing outside stirs the occupants of a small forest cabin.

51)　The sounds through the trees as the summer breezes blow the branches, but will Katy remember?

_____
_____
_____
_____
_____
_____
_____
_____
_____
_____
_____
_____
_____
_____
_____
_____
_____
_____
_____
_____
_____
_____
_____
_____
_____
_____
_____
_____
_____
_____
_____

Chapter Three – Murder

In these stories, you have the freedom to use your imagination to lead up to the murder and to make the reasons for the murder logical to the readers, keeping them in suspense by clever plot work.

52)   There are no real suspects but Inspector Miles has a gut feeling. Will it lead to the apprehension of Jenny's killer?

_____
_____
_____
_____
_____
_____
_____
_____
_____
_____
_____
_____
_____
_____
_____
_____
_____
_____
_____
_____
_____
_____
_____
_____

53)   You can't walk down on the beach at night. They were warned, but they took no notice.

_____
_____
_____
_____
_____
_____
_____
_____
_____
_____
_____
_____
_____
_____
_____
_____
_____
_____
_____
_____
_____
_____
_____
_____
_____
_____
_____
_____
_____
_____
_____
_____

54) Murders on campus – but will the murderer be who they all suspect?

55)   Being away from home is scary enough, but when a stranger leads you to an alleyway, what awaits you?

_____
_____
_____
_____
_____
_____
_____
_____
_____
_____
_____
_____
_____
_____
_____
_____
_____
_____
_____
_____
_____
_____
_____
_____
_____
_____
_____
_____
_____
_____
_____
_____
_____
_____
_____
_____
_____

56)   Two guns, both fired from but only one body. How come?

_____
_____
_____
_____
_____
_____
_____
_____
_____
_____
_____
_____
_____
_____
_____
_____
_____
_____
_____
_____
_____
_____
_____
_____
_____
_____
_____
_____
_____
_____

57)   When a husband reacts violently to police questioning, does this indicate that he killed his wife?

_____
_____
_____
_____
_____
_____
_____
_____
_____
_____
_____
_____
_____
_____
_____
_____
_____
_____
_____
_____
_____
_____
_____
_____
_____
_____
_____
_____
_____
_____
_____
_____
_____
_____
_____
_____
_____

58) An old lady who lives alone, but one who was sitting on a fortune. Who knew?

_____

_____

_____

_____

_____

_____

_____

_____

_____

_____

_____

_____

_____

_____

_____

_____

_____

_____

_____

_____

_____

_____

_____

_____

_____

_____

_____

_____

_____

_____

_____

_____

_____

_____

59)   The overdose was fatal, though all signs showed the police that the death was foul play.

_____

_____

_____

_____

_____

_____

_____

_____

_____

_____

_____

_____

_____

_____

_____

_____

_____

_____

_____

_____

_____

_____

_____

_____

_____

_____

_____

_____

_____

_____

_____

_____

60)   An accidental fall or an intentional act? When her body was found at the foot of the hotel building, questions were asked.

---

61)   The killer always leaves a calling card, though this time, there was no calling card left. A copycat or the real killer?

_____
_____
_____
_____
_____
_____
_____
_____
_____
_____
_____
_____
_____
_____
_____
_____
_____
_____
_____
_____
_____
_____
_____
_____
_____
_____
_____
_____
_____
_____
_____
_____
_____
_____
_____
_____
_____
_____

62)   When Alice finds her husband dead in the garage of their home, her reactions are a little baffling.

_____
_____
_____
_____
_____
_____
_____
_____
_____
_____
_____
_____
_____
_____
_____
_____
_____
_____
_____
_____
_____
_____
_____
_____
_____
_____
_____
_____
_____
_____
_____
_____
_____
_____
_____

63) She has the gun. She feels the hatred, though will she pull the trigger?

---

64)   His body was slumped over the banister of their holiday villa, though all signs of life were gone. Who left the large wound on his head?

_____
_____
_____
_____
_____
_____
_____
_____
_____
_____
_____
_____
_____
_____
_____
_____
_____
_____
_____
_____
_____
_____
_____
_____
_____
_____
_____
_____
_____
_____
_____
_____
_____

65)   Dead and buried, but still the torment in Jane's mind stops her from moving on.

_____

_____

_____

_____

_____

_____

_____

_____

_____

_____

_____

_____

_____

_____

_____

_____

_____

_____

_____

_____

_____

_____

_____

_____

_____

_____

_____

_____

_____

_____

_____

_____

_____

_____

_____

_____

Chapter Four – Unrequited love

66)   Polly feels her attempts to gain his attention are falling on deaf ears, until he hints otherwise.

_____
_____
_____
_____
_____
_____
_____
_____
_____
_____
_____
_____
_____
_____
_____
_____
_____
_____
_____
_____
_____
_____
_____
_____
_____
_____
_____
_____
_____
_____
_____
_____
_____

67)   Jason has worked on the farm most of his life. When Amy's husband dies, can Jason take his place?

_____
_____
_____
_____
_____
_____
_____
_____
_____
_____
_____
_____
_____
_____
_____
_____
_____
_____
_____
_____
_____
_____
_____
_____
_____
_____
_____
_____
_____
_____
_____
_____
_____
_____
_____
_____
_____

68)   The bitter and twisted Petra admits her love for the one man who can destroy her.

69)   Sisters, Claire and Suzanne are in love with the same man, though which will he choose and how will the sister left out revenge his rejection?

_____
_____
_____
_____
_____
_____
_____
_____
_____
_____
_____
_____
_____
_____
_____
_____
_____
_____
_____
_____
_____
_____
_____
_____
_____
_____
_____
_____
_____
_____
_____
_____
_____
_____
_____
_____
_____
_____
_____
_____
_____
_____

70)   Lady Amelia Forster is rejected by the man she loves. Her reaction surprises everyone.

_____
_____
_____
_____
_____
_____
_____
_____
_____
_____
_____
_____
_____
_____
_____
_____
_____
_____
_____
_____
_____
_____
_____
_____
_____
_____
_____
_____
_____
_____
_____
_____
_____

71)   When a maidservant falls for the son of the Master of the house, she knows this cannot be. How will she cope?

_____

_____

_____

_____

_____

_____

_____

_____

_____

_____

_____

_____

_____

_____

_____

_____

_____

_____

_____

_____

_____

_____

_____

_____

_____

_____

_____

_____

_____

_____

_____

_____

_____

_____

_____

_____

_____

_____

_____

_____

_____

72)   Hell hath no fury like a woman scorned. Rejected and alone, Alice seeks her revenge.

_____
_____
_____
_____
_____
_____
_____
_____
_____
_____
_____
_____
_____
_____
_____
_____
_____
_____
_____
_____
_____
_____
_____
_____
_____
_____
_____
_____
_____
_____
_____
_____
_____
_____

73)   The impossible dream. Gemma knows he is untouchable though circumstances work in her favor.

74)   He is rich. He is eligible, but he isn't interested. How does Kathy change his mind?

_____
_____
_____
_____
_____
_____
_____
_____
_____
_____
_____
_____
_____
_____
_____
_____
_____
_____
_____
_____
_____
_____
_____
_____
_____
_____
_____
_____
_____
_____
_____
_____
_____

Chapter Five – Stories of Friendship

75)   They have been friends all of their lives, though George steps in between their friendship and it changes the dynamic forever.

_____

_____

_____

_____

_____

_____

_____

_____

_____

_____

_____

_____

_____

_____

_____

_____

_____

_____

_____

_____

_____

_____

_____

_____

_____

_____

_____

_____

_____

_____

_____

_____

_____

_____

_____

_____

76)   Chad and Wills have grown up together and are now in their mid-thirties, but what happens to divide that friendship and make them hate each other?

_____

_____

_____

_____

_____

_____

_____

_____

_____

_____

_____

_____

_____

_____

_____

_____

_____

_____

_____

_____

_____

_____

_____

_____

_____

_____

_____

_____

_____

77)   Emily has everything that Kay ever wanted, but does she? As Emily delves deeper, she finds secrets that spell out the unhappiness of her friend's life.

_____

_____

_____

_____

_____

_____

_____

_____

_____

_____

_____

_____

_____

_____

_____

_____

_____

_____

_____

_____

_____

_____

_____

_____

_____

_____

_____

_____

_____

_____

_____

_____

_____

_____

_____

78)   Can Jeremy ever trust his friend again? Lies hurt and too many have been told. However, perhaps Jeremy's reasons were justified.

_____
_____
_____
_____
_____
_____
_____
_____
_____
_____
_____
_____
_____
_____
_____
_____
_____
_____
_____
_____
_____
_____
_____
_____
_____
_____
_____
_____
_____
_____
_____
_____
_____
_____
_____
_____
_____

79)   When Larry is injured in a car accident, can he forgive his friend for his drunk driving?

_____

_____

_____

_____

_____

_____

_____

_____

_____

_____

_____

_____

_____

_____

_____

_____

_____

_____

_____

_____

_____

_____

_____

_____

_____

_____

_____

_____

_____

_____

_____

_____

_____

_____

_____

_____

_____

_____

_____

_____

_____

_____

_____

_____

_____

80)   Happy go lucky Lilian soon finds that her luck has run out. Can Jade help her get beyond this sad period in her life?

_____
_____
_____
_____
_____
_____
_____
_____
_____
_____
_____
_____
_____
_____
_____
_____
_____
_____
_____
_____
_____
_____
_____
_____
_____
_____
_____
_____
_____
_____
_____
_____
_____
_____
_____
_____
_____
_____
_____

81)   He isn't real. Mrs. Kelly made him up but her best friend wants to know why.

_____

_____

_____

_____

_____

_____

_____

_____

_____

_____

_____

_____

_____

_____

_____

_____

_____

_____

_____

_____

_____

_____

_____

_____

_____

_____

_____

_____

_____

_____

_____

_____

_____

_____

_____

_____

_____

82)   The best gift in the world is the gift of friendship. However, what happens when it comes with strings attached?

_____
_____
_____
_____
_____
_____
_____
_____
_____
_____
_____
_____
_____
_____
_____
_____
_____
_____
_____
_____
_____
_____
_____
_____
_____
_____
_____
_____
_____
_____
_____
_____
_____
_____
_____
_____
_____
_____
_____
_____
_____
_____
_____
_____
_____
_____

83)   Yvonne tries to help Kerry get over his drinking problem, but the deeper she gets, the harder it is for her to break away.

84)   What happens when the ties of friendship drag you into a criminal life? Benny finds out the cost of friendship.

_____
_____
_____
_____
_____
_____
_____
_____
_____
_____
_____
_____
_____
_____
_____
_____
_____
_____
_____
_____
_____
_____
_____
_____
_____
_____
_____
_____
_____
_____
_____
_____
_____

Chapter Six – Learning about Narrative – Stories of People

When you want to write what people are saying to each other, the speech goes into speech marks. Often people find it hard to know where the punctuation goes and how to make conversation a useful tool for making characters come to life.

"Hi," said Kelly.

"I wish I lived in a house like yours."

In the next batch of stories, try to use narrative several times during the story. Remember to leave a certain amount of guesswork to the readers so that they are always anxious to turn the next page.

85)   Janine wants to dominate the relationship. With clever words, she persuades Lyle to step away from being in charge.

_____
_____
_____
_____
_____
_____
_____
_____
_____
_____
_____
_____
_____
_____

86)   Lawrie and Sue's relationship comes to breaking point when Sue tells Lawrie something he can't dismiss.

_____

_____

_____

_____

_____

_____

_____

_____

_____

_____

_____

_____

_____

_____

_____

_____

_____

_____

_____

_____

_____

_____

_____

_____

_____

_____

_____

_____

_____

_____

_____

_____

_____

_____

87)   Grampa Willis wants to convey something to his wife on his deathbed, though what will the impact be on his wife?

_____
_____
_____
_____
_____
_____
_____
_____
_____
_____
_____
_____
_____
_____
_____
_____
_____
_____
_____
_____
_____
_____
_____
_____
_____
_____
_____
_____
_____
_____
_____
_____
_____
_____
_____
_____
_____
_____
_____
_____
_____
_____
_____

88)   Will and Tom need to get past their differences and try to help their parents rebuild their lives after fire destroys their home.

89)   The anger, the angst and the irony of a relationship with a drunk.

_____
_____
_____
_____
_____
_____
_____
_____
_____
_____
_____
_____
_____
_____
_____
_____
_____
_____
_____
_____
_____
_____
_____
_____
_____
_____
_____
_____
_____
_____
_____
_____
_____
_____
_____
_____

90)   Max wants to tell her about his secret, though Julia isn't the easiest person when it comes to listening.

_____

_____

_____

_____

_____

_____

_____

_____

_____

_____

_____

_____

_____

_____

_____

_____

_____

_____

_____

_____

_____

_____

_____

_____

_____

_____

_____

_____

_____

_____

_____

_____

_____

91)   The old man who lives at Number 92 Willis Street has a battle with his neighbor that ends in tragedy.

92)   Breaking the ice, two travelers on a train find they have more in common than they first supposed.

_____
_____
_____
_____
_____
_____
_____
_____
_____
_____
_____
_____
_____
_____
_____
_____
_____
_____
_____
_____
_____
_____
_____
_____
_____
_____
_____
_____
_____
_____
_____
_____
_____
_____
_____
_____
_____
_____
_____
_____

93)   The laughter between friends is suddenly brought to a halt when a secret is revealed that hurts Gemma to the core.

_____
_____
_____
_____
_____
_____
_____
_____
_____
_____
_____
_____
_____
_____
_____
_____
_____
_____
_____
_____
_____
_____
_____
_____
_____
_____
_____
_____
_____
_____
_____
_____
_____
_____

94)   Henry and John compete within the working environment, and when one of them gets promoted, the other is left with self-esteem problems.

_____
_____
_____
_____
_____
_____
_____
_____
_____
_____
_____
_____
_____
_____
_____
_____
_____
_____
_____
_____
_____
_____
_____
_____
_____
_____
_____
_____
_____
_____
_____
_____
_____
_____

95)   Hayleigh is fed up of being used and decides to do something about it. Will Amelia understand?

_____
_____
_____
_____
_____
_____
_____
_____
_____
_____
_____
_____
_____
_____
_____
_____
_____
_____
_____
_____
_____
_____
_____
_____
_____
_____
_____
_____
_____
_____
_____
_____
_____

96)   Things come to a head when Jane confronts her mother about the lack of care her mother showed in her childhood. Then the truth emerges.

_____

_____

_____

_____

_____

_____

_____

_____

_____

_____

_____

_____

_____

_____

_____

_____

_____

_____

_____

_____

_____

_____

_____

_____

_____

_____

_____

_____

_____

_____

_____

_____

_____

_____

_____

Chapter Seven – Adjectives

As a writer, you will know that an adjective is a describing word. Close your eyes after reading the prompt and describe what you see making your story come to life in the mind of readers. Bring atmosphere to your work and try to picture the image in your mind's eye before describing it.

97)   A spooky night in the forest. Will the werewolf find his prey? Or will Angelica be able to escape the threat?

_____
_____
_____
_____
_____
_____
_____
_____
_____
_____
_____
_____
_____
_____
_____
_____
_____
_____
_____
_____
_____
_____
_____
_____

98)   Summer of 1967 – Freedom, music and love. Though Jake has been called up and may never return.

_____
_____
_____
_____
_____
_____
_____
_____
_____
_____
_____
_____
_____
_____
_____
_____
_____
_____
_____
_____
_____
_____
_____
_____
_____
_____
_____
_____
_____
_____
_____
_____
_____
_____
_____

99)   The ladies are gathered in the sitting room, waiting for the reading of their father's will. However, not all young ladies get what they expect.

100) The meadows are filled with wild flowers. Aaron and Sara are going against their Amish traditions and meeting in secret.

_____
_____
_____
_____
_____
_____
_____
_____
_____
_____
_____
_____
_____
_____
_____
_____
_____
_____
_____
_____
_____
_____
_____
_____
_____
_____
_____
_____
_____
_____
_____
_____
_____
_____
_____
_____
_____

101)   Class discrimination – In Victorian London, the downstairs maid falls victim to the folly of her Master's wishes.

102) She is young, elegant and attractive, though he is a rough cut diamond. Can he persuade her?

_____

_____

_____

_____

_____

_____

_____

_____

_____

_____

_____

_____

_____

_____

_____

_____

_____

_____

_____

_____

_____

_____

_____

_____

_____

_____

_____

_____

_____

_____

_____

_____

_____

_____

_____

_____

_____

_____

_____

_____

103) The garden holds secrets, but as Janine digs deeper, what she finds is something extraordinary.

_____
_____
_____
_____
_____
_____
_____
_____
_____
_____
_____
_____
_____
_____
_____
_____
_____
_____
_____
_____
_____
_____
_____
_____
_____
_____
_____
_____
_____
_____
_____
_____
_____

Chapter Eight – Fantasy

In these stories, you create the characters, based on the writing prompt. The sky is your limit. Try to imagine this fantasy world and the characters who live in it.

104)   The maze – Jamie is lost in the maize but can anyone help him to get back to familiar territory?

_____
_____
_____
_____
_____
_____
_____
_____
_____
_____
_____
_____
_____
_____
_____
_____
_____
_____
_____
_____
_____
_____
_____
_____

105) In a land under the sea, but how you get there is secret. When Patricia discovers, can she ever come home again?

106) The scroll in the old church gives all the clues, in a language long since replaced, though Alicia has learned the symbols through her archeological classes.

_____

_____

_____

_____

_____

_____

_____

_____

_____

_____

_____

_____

_____

_____

_____

_____

_____

_____

_____

_____

_____

_____

_____

_____

_____

_____

_____

_____

_____

_____

107)   The treasures of the elders are held upon an island, though will Kate and Will be able to locate them?

_____
_____
_____
_____
_____
_____
_____
_____
_____
_____
_____
_____
_____
_____
_____
_____
_____
_____
_____
_____
_____
_____
_____
_____
_____
_____
_____
_____
_____
_____
_____
_____
_____
_____
_____
_____

108) The old man holds a bird in his hand. The way that the bird sings determines the outcome. Only Paul knows the secret.

_____
_____
_____
_____
_____
_____
_____
_____
_____
_____
_____
_____
_____
_____
_____
_____
_____
_____
_____
_____
_____
_____
_____
_____
_____
_____
_____
_____
_____
_____

109) Melony finds her way through the black hole and discovers something very interesting at the other end.

_____
_____
_____
_____
_____
_____
_____
_____
_____
_____
_____
_____
_____
_____
_____
_____
_____
_____
_____
_____
_____
_____
_____
_____
_____
_____
_____
_____
_____
_____
_____
_____

110)   Can you send messages to another dimension? Larry thinks you can, but needs to prove it.

111)   The boat pulls into the island of Mull and as it does so, Jack notices the cloud hanging over Cowdry Castle. Is this a sign?

_____
_____
_____
_____
_____
_____
_____
_____
_____
_____
_____
_____
_____
_____
_____
_____
_____
_____
_____
_____
_____
_____
_____
_____
_____
_____
_____
_____
_____
_____
_____
_____
_____
_____
_____
_____
_____
_____

112)   The wolves in the forest are hungry for blood, though Kyle and Ian have to escape. Can they find their way through the tunnels to freedom?

_____

_____

_____

_____

_____

_____

_____

_____

_____

_____

_____

_____

_____

_____

_____

_____

_____

_____

_____

_____

_____

_____

_____

_____

_____

_____

_____

_____

_____

_____

_____

_____

113)   Ilk is not interested in human excuses. His response to Jillian and her brother turn their worlds upside down.

_____

_____

_____

_____

_____

_____

_____

_____

_____

_____

_____

_____

_____

_____

_____

_____

_____

_____

_____

_____

_____

_____

_____

_____

_____

_____

_____

_____

_____

_____

_____

_____

_____

114)   Becky is afraid of the dark, though the dark holds secrets that can free her of this fear.

_____
_____
_____
_____
_____
_____
_____
_____
_____
_____
_____
_____
_____
_____
_____
_____
_____
_____
_____
_____
_____
_____
_____
_____
_____
_____
_____
_____
_____
_____
_____
_____
_____
_____
_____

115)   In the hills of Katmandu, a small tribe of people show travelers the way to escape their own destiny.

116) Sara holds the keys to the city, though the keyhole will not take the key. Will she discover the other way to enter the city?

_____

_____

_____

_____

_____

_____

_____

_____

_____

_____

_____

_____

_____

_____

_____

_____

_____

_____

_____

_____

_____

_____

_____

_____

_____

_____

_____

_____

_____

_____

_____

_____

_____

_____

117)   Stuck in a time warp, James regrets the actions of his life and can only move forward by showing true repentance.

_____
_____
_____
_____
_____
_____
_____
_____
_____
_____
_____
_____
_____
_____
_____
_____
_____
_____
_____
_____
_____
_____
_____
_____
_____
_____
_____
_____
_____
_____
_____
_____
_____
_____
_____
_____
_____

Chapter Nine – Erotica

Erotica is a popular genre of fiction that borders upon the sexual without actually delving into the activity. The descriptive process is very important and it's more about what is not said than what is drawn out into a clear picture. Use these prompts to come up with tempting and tantalizing stories.

118)   Harry Brown is a typical bachelor – rich, good looking and very eligible, but how will Helen get him interested?

_____
_____
_____
_____
_____
_____
_____
_____
_____
_____
_____
_____
_____
_____
_____
_____
_____
_____
_____
_____
_____
_____
_____

119)   The sexual feelings encountered by Richard as he makes his way through his mid-life crisis change everything Richard ever held dear.

120)   Falling in love with a ballerina, dance is the only way that she can show him the difference between making love and simply having sex. George finds his life changed forever when she pulls him into her clutches.

_____
_____
_____
_____
_____
_____
_____
_____
_____
_____
_____
_____
_____
_____
_____
_____
_____
_____
_____
_____
_____
_____
_____
_____
_____
_____
_____
_____
_____
_____
_____

121)   Patricia falls for the gardener, though against her parents approval, manages to keep her affair under wraps.

122) The threesome – real or fantasy? Two friends explore their sexual feelings for one particularly good looking man.

_____
_____
_____
_____
_____
_____
_____
_____
_____
_____
_____
_____
_____
_____
_____
_____
_____
_____
_____
_____
_____
_____
_____
_____
_____
_____
_____
_____
_____
_____
_____
_____
_____
_____
_____
_____
_____

123)   She wanted a white wedding, though what she got was far from what she expected.

_____

_____

_____

_____

_____

_____

_____

_____

_____

_____

_____

_____

_____

_____

_____

_____

_____

_____

_____

_____

_____

_____

_____

_____

_____

_____

_____

_____

_____

_____

_____

_____

_____

_____

_____

_____

_____

_____

124)   The words he said stayed in her mind for years, until one day she had the chance to answer him.

_____

_____

_____

_____

_____

_____

_____

_____

_____

_____

_____

_____

_____

_____

_____

_____

_____

_____

_____

_____

_____

_____

_____

_____

_____

_____

_____

_____

_____

_____

125) Sometimes there is no need for words, but the actions, the implications and the allure are enough.

_____
_____
_____
_____
_____
_____
_____
_____
_____
_____
_____
_____
_____
_____
_____
_____
_____
_____
_____
_____
_____
_____
_____
_____
_____
_____
_____
_____
_____
_____
_____
_____
_____
_____
_____

126)   Two souls each at their own side of the world pull each other into a web of deceit and fantasy.

_____
_____
_____
_____
_____
_____
_____
_____
_____
_____
_____
_____
_____
_____
_____
_____
_____
_____
_____
_____
_____
_____
_____
_____
_____
_____
_____
_____
_____
_____
_____
_____
_____
_____
_____
_____

Chapter Ten – Science Fiction

In this section, you can choose from the two prompts given and use descriptive qualities within your writing as well as imaginary scenarios from the future.

127)   When time travel takes Gregory back to another time, he needs to escape the reality of finding out the truth about his parents.

_____
_____
_____
_____
_____
_____
_____
_____
_____
_____
_____
_____
_____
_____
_____
_____
_____
_____
_____
_____
_____
_____
_____
_____
_____
_____
_____
_____
_____
_____
_____
_____

128)   Robots are in every home, though the robot that the Nicholson family buy comes with surprise abilities.

129) Heading a team of investigators, Terry finds that the scientists have hidden all evidence needed to prove his innocence.

_____
_____
_____
_____
_____
_____
_____
_____
_____
_____
_____
_____
_____
_____
_____
_____
_____
_____
_____
_____
_____
_____
_____
_____
_____
_____
_____
_____
_____
_____
_____
_____
_____
_____

130) Eleanor's parents need to medicate her to get her to behave within the confines of acceptable behavior, though she escapes into another world.

_____
_____
_____
_____
_____
_____
_____
_____
_____
_____
_____
_____
_____
_____
_____
_____
_____
_____
_____
_____
_____
_____
_____
_____
_____
_____
_____
_____
_____
_____
_____
_____

131)   Lawrence cannot escape the telepathic abilities of his brother.

132)   The stars are aligned and this means the end of the world. However, there is one chance of saving the world from destruction.

_____

_____

_____

_____

_____

_____

_____

_____

_____

_____

_____

_____

_____

_____

_____

_____

_____

_____

_____

_____

_____

_____

_____

_____

_____

_____

_____

_____

_____

_____

_____

_____

_____

_____

_____

Chapter Eleven – Historical Literature

133)   Sir James Halway is to meet his rival for a duel over the love of Lady Margaret.

_____

_____

_____

_____

_____

_____

_____

_____

_____

_____

_____

_____

_____

_____

_____

_____

_____

_____

_____

_____

_____

_____

_____

_____

_____

_____

_____

_____

_____

134) Ellen is in a woman's prison in Victorian England and cannot escape even though protesting her innocence.

_____
_____
_____
_____
_____
_____
_____
_____
_____
_____
_____
_____
_____
_____
_____
_____
_____
_____
_____
_____
_____
_____
_____
_____
_____
_____
_____
_____
_____
_____
_____
_____
_____
_____

135) The carriage awaits, but where will it take her. Emelia has been sent away from her family in disgrace since becoming pregnant by the family groom.

_____
_____
_____
_____
_____
_____
_____
_____
_____
_____
_____
_____
_____
_____
_____
_____
_____
_____
_____
_____
_____
_____
_____
_____
_____
_____
_____
_____
_____
_____

136)   Peter is about to inherit his father's riches, though the will imposes a restriction that he needs to be married. How will he overcome this?

_____

_____

_____

_____

_____

_____

_____

_____

_____

_____

_____

_____

_____

_____

_____

_____

_____

_____

_____

_____

_____

_____

_____

_____

_____

_____

_____

_____

_____

_____

_____

_____

Chapter Twelve – Colors

We all know how to describe basic colors, but in these stories, subtlety is needed to describe whatever comes to mind when reading the prompts.

137)   Janine's hair is a wonderful shade of golden, though caught on canvas, the artist misses the nuances that make her original.

_____
_____
_____
_____
_____
_____
_____
_____
_____
_____
_____
_____
_____
_____
_____
_____
_____
_____
_____
_____
_____
_____
_____
_____
_____
_____
_____
_____
_____
_____

138)   The color of the sky at night is enchanting. As Rebecca and Ewan make their way on horseback toward their future, the night sky enfolds them.

_____
_____
_____
_____
_____
_____
_____
_____
_____
_____
_____
_____
_____
_____
_____
_____
_____
_____
_____
_____
_____
_____
_____
_____
_____
_____
_____
_____

139)   The sea has several nuances. When calm, the blueness or greenness of the sea is tempting, though in storms, the color changes.

_____
_____
_____
_____
_____
_____
_____
_____
_____
_____
_____
_____
_____
_____
_____
_____
_____
_____
_____
_____
_____
_____
_____
_____
_____
_____
_____
_____
_____
_____
_____
_____
_____
_____
_____
_____
_____
_____

140) The colors of the rainbow dance across the sky, and as Peter proposes to Gaynor, the rainbow becomes a significant part of their love story.

_____

_____

_____

_____

_____

_____

_____

_____

_____

_____

_____

_____

_____

_____

_____

_____

_____

_____

_____

_____

_____

_____

_____

_____

_____

_____

_____

_____

_____

_____

_____

_____

_____

_____

141)   New York Fashion week and the color of the year is Yellow. Against the backdrop of the walkway, Jemima shows its true meaning of jealousy and deceit.

_____

_____

_____

_____

_____

_____

_____

_____

_____

_____

_____

_____

_____

_____

_____

_____

_____

_____

_____

_____

_____

_____

_____

_____

_____

_____

_____

_____

_____

_____

_____

_____

_____

_____

_____

142) The flowers in the garden have begun to bloom, but underneath the flowerbed, hides a secret only to be discovered by he who looks.

_____
_____
_____
_____
_____
_____
_____
_____
_____
_____
_____
_____
_____
_____
_____
_____
_____
_____
_____
_____
_____
_____
_____
_____
_____
_____
_____
_____
_____
_____

143)   It's time to sleep the dream of death, as the light plays games upon the wall of Martha's bedroom.

144) The colors of the city, looking down from the rooftop where Lily and Malcolm discover their mutual love of the city lights.

_____

_____

_____

_____

_____

_____

_____

_____

_____

_____

_____

_____

_____

_____

_____

_____

_____

_____

_____

_____

_____

_____

_____

_____

_____

_____

_____

_____

_____

_____

_____

_____

_____

_____

_____

Chapter Thirteen – Contemporary Fiction

145) In the world of art, Pamela intends to make her mark, but will she be able to persuade her agent?

_____
_____
_____
_____
_____
_____
_____
_____
_____
_____
_____
_____
_____
_____
_____
_____
_____
_____
_____
_____
_____
_____
_____
_____
_____
_____
_____
_____
_____

146) Being alone in a darkened world, Petra finds her way.

_____
_____
_____
_____
_____
_____
_____
_____
_____
_____
_____
_____
_____
_____
_____
_____
_____
_____
_____
_____
_____
_____
_____
_____
_____
_____
_____
_____
_____
_____
_____
_____
_____
_____
_____
_____

147) Through yoga classes, Amy finds balance in her life.

148) When Peter changes his role in a mystery TV series, his whole life changes.

_____
_____
_____
_____
_____
_____
_____
_____
_____
_____
_____
_____
_____
_____
_____
_____
_____
_____
_____
_____
_____
_____
_____
_____
_____
_____
_____
_____
_____
_____
_____
_____
_____
_____
_____
_____

149)   Patiently waiting for something to happen in her life, Olive makes a wish upon a clover leaf and a new life unfolds.

_____
_____
_____
_____
_____
_____
_____
_____
_____
_____
_____
_____
_____
_____
_____
_____
_____
_____
_____
_____
_____
_____
_____
_____
_____
_____
_____
_____
_____
_____
_____
_____
_____
_____
_____
_____
_____

150) Michael is faced with a life-changing decision to make – to do or to die?

_____

_____

_____

_____

_____

_____

_____

_____

_____

_____

_____

_____

_____

_____

_____

_____

_____

_____

_____

_____

_____

_____

_____

_____

_____

_____

_____

_____

_____

_____

_____

151) Running toward nowhere, Lawrence finds his legs have given way and the road ahead has disappeared over the horizon.

152)   Wonderful ideas and dreams, stopped in their track by reality.

153)   Life in old world Japan and Isiko finds that escape is impossible from her destiny as a geisha.

154) The door to nowhere – where people must face their fears.

_____
_____
_____
_____
_____
_____
_____
_____
_____
_____
_____
_____
_____
_____
_____
_____
_____
_____
_____
_____
_____
_____
_____
_____
_____
_____
_____
_____
_____
_____
_____
_____

155)   The gift that keeps giving – Emily holds it in her hand.

_____
_____
_____
_____
_____
_____
_____
_____
_____
_____
_____
_____
_____
_____
_____
_____
_____
_____
_____
_____
_____
_____
_____
_____
_____
_____
_____
_____

156)   There are no doors, no windows – just darkness, though somehow Jules finds his escape.

_____
_____
_____
_____
_____
_____
_____
_____
_____
_____
_____
_____
_____
_____
_____
_____
_____
_____
_____
_____
_____
_____
_____
_____
_____
_____
_____
_____
_____
_____
_____

157)   The woman in the picture is familiar to Giles, but then he remembers where he knows her from. What good will it do him?

_____
_____
_____
_____
_____
_____
_____
_____
_____
_____
_____
_____
_____
_____
_____
_____
_____
_____
_____
_____
_____
_____
_____
_____
_____
_____
_____
_____
_____
_____
_____
_____
_____
_____

Chapter Fourteen – Love Stories

These can be tragic, happy ever after stories or stories that hold promise. However, each must be original and well thought out.

158)   Carrie is afraid of Michael telling her husband about her infidelity.

_____
_____
_____
_____
_____
_____
_____
_____
_____
_____
_____
_____
_____
_____
_____
_____
_____
_____
_____
_____
_____
_____
_____
_____
_____
_____
_____
_____
_____
_____
_____

163) Against impossible odds, Kerry and June find their happy ever after.

_____
_____
_____
_____
_____
_____
_____
_____
_____
_____
_____
_____
_____
_____
_____
_____
_____
_____

164) Fourteen years of loving him and now he is free at last. How will Linda win him over?

_____
_____
_____
_____
_____
_____
_____
_____
_____
_____
_____
_____
_____
_____
_____
_____
_____

165) A poor artist, a beautiful woman and the perfect love.

_____
_____
_____
_____
_____
_____
_____
_____
_____
_____
_____
_____
_____
_____
_____
_____
_____
_____

166) The wedding day, but is it as perfect as they hoped?

_____
_____
_____
_____
_____
_____
_____
_____
_____
_____
_____
_____
_____
_____
_____
_____
_____

167) Paula falls in love with her tutor though will she be able to sustain forbidden love?

_____

_____

_____

_____

_____

_____

_____

_____

_____

_____

_____

_____

_____

_____

_____

_____

168) George knows that if he doesn't tell her now, he may never get another chance.

_____

_____

_____

_____

_____

_____

_____

_____

_____

_____

_____

_____

_____

_____

169)   Loving against all odds, Jane battles her family but retains her loved one.

_____
_____
_____
_____
_____
_____
_____
_____
_____
_____
_____
_____
_____
_____
_____

170)   The text said "Tonight?" Jasmine said "Yes" but what followed changed her life forever.

_____
_____
_____
_____
_____
_____
_____
_____
_____
_____
_____
_____
_____
_____

171)   He promised her the world and took her world and destroyed it.

_____

_____

_____

_____

_____

_____

_____

_____

_____

_____

_____

_____

_____

_____

_____

_____

172)   She was from a different class, though they made it through times of struggle.

_____

_____

_____

_____

_____

_____

_____

_____

_____

_____

_____

_____

_____

_____

_____

_____

173) He was black, she was white, their love as sweet as coffee with cream.

Leave Us a Review!

www.LeaveHonest.Review/365Prompts

Thank you for all the support!
You keep my family fed and happy!

We couldn't do it without you!

www.tmcrane.org/101kids

Chapter Fifteen – Plot Scenarios

In this chapter, we deal with developing your plot. The prompt will give you a hint, but you need to come up with a great plot with at least one moment of drama and surprise.

174)   The killing at Marystone Mansion – who dunnit?

_____

_____

_____

_____

_____

_____

_____

_____

_____

_____

_____

_____

_____

_____

_____

_____

_____

_____

_____

_____

_____

_____

_____

_____

_____

_____

175) Andy can't make his mind up – was his wife unfaithful or was she trying to protect him?

_____

_____

_____

_____

_____

_____

_____

_____

_____

_____

_____

_____

_____

_____

_____

_____

_____

_____

_____

_____

_____

_____

_____

_____

_____

_____

_____

_____

_____

176)   Amber knows that her brother has found out about her affair and is about to tell her parents. How can she stop him?

_____
_____
_____
_____
_____
_____
_____
_____
_____
_____
_____
_____
_____
_____
_____
_____
_____
_____
_____
_____
_____
_____
_____
_____
_____
_____
_____
_____
_____
_____
_____
_____
_____
_____
_____
_____

177)   Holding a gun to his head is the only way Jennifer has of saying "No"

_____
_____
_____
_____
_____
_____
_____
_____
_____
_____
_____
_____
_____
_____
_____
_____
_____
_____
_____
_____
_____
_____
_____
_____
_____
_____
_____
_____
_____
_____
_____
_____
_____
_____
_____
_____
_____

178)   Single parents, both with kids, get together but find that it's not the wonderful life they imagined.

179)   Lilian has burns on her arms from a childhood fire, but wants to pay for plastic surgery. However, everything goes wrong.

180) Mrs. Kelly isn't as innocent as she seems. She has ill intentions, but will she get away with it?

_____
_____
_____
_____
_____
_____
_____
_____
_____
_____
_____
_____
_____
_____
_____
_____
_____
_____
_____
_____
_____
_____
_____
_____
_____
_____
_____
_____
_____
_____
_____
_____
_____
_____
_____
_____
_____
_____
_____
_____
_____
_____
_____
_____
_____
_____
_____
_____

181) Billy sees his life destroyed when his identity is stolen. How will he get it back?

_____

_____

_____

_____

_____

_____

_____

_____

_____

_____

_____

_____

_____

_____

_____

_____

_____

_____

_____

_____

_____

_____

_____

_____

_____

_____

_____

_____

_____

_____

_____

_____

_____

_____

_____

_____

_____

182) Mary's mother has deceived her father? Will she tell him?

183)   Patricia's father is in jail. He is innocent and she knows it.

_____

_____

_____

_____

_____

_____

_____

_____

_____

_____

_____

_____

_____

_____

_____

_____

_____

_____

_____

_____

_____

_____

_____

_____

_____

_____

_____

_____

_____

184)   Abbey has to tell the truth but is afraid she will lose her husband.

_____
_____
_____
_____
_____
_____
_____
_____
_____
_____
_____
_____
_____
_____
_____
_____
_____
_____
_____
_____
_____
_____
_____
_____
_____
_____
_____
_____
_____
_____
_____
_____
_____
_____

185) Kerry is stumped. He knows that he did wrong, but can he make it right?

_____

_____

_____

_____

_____

_____

_____

_____

_____

_____

_____

_____

_____

_____

_____

_____

_____

_____

_____

_____

_____

_____

_____

_____

_____

_____

_____

_____

_____

_____

_____

_____

186) Mrs. Jennings finds evidence of foul play, but who will listen?

_____
_____
_____
_____
_____
_____
_____
_____
_____
_____
_____
_____
_____
_____
_____
_____
_____
_____

187) How will Kate persuade her husband that divorce is the best solution?

_____
_____
_____
_____
_____
_____
_____
_____
_____
_____
_____
_____
_____
_____
_____
_____
_____
_____

Chapter Sixteen – Mystery

With a mystery story, it's important to keep surprises up your sleeve. Try your hand with these.

188)   The key fit into the briefcase, though the secrets held within would change Emily's life forever.

_____
_____
_____
_____
_____
_____
_____
_____
_____
_____
_____
_____
_____
_____
_____
_____
_____
_____
_____
_____
_____
_____
_____
_____
_____
_____

189) Whose is the black car that appears next door at 11 at night and then disappears by morning?

_____
_____
_____
_____
_____
_____
_____
_____
_____
_____
_____
_____
_____
_____
_____
_____
_____
_____
_____
_____
_____
_____
_____
_____
_____
_____
_____
_____
_____
_____
_____
_____
_____
_____
_____
_____
_____
_____
_____
_____
_____
_____
_____

190) The book holds the clues, though Kelly needs to decipher the code.

_____
_____
_____
_____
_____
_____
_____
_____
_____
_____
_____
_____
_____
_____
_____
_____
_____
_____
_____
_____
_____
_____
_____
_____
_____
_____
_____
_____
_____
_____
_____
_____

191) He looks like James, but James is dead or is he?

192) Angelica comes to grips with more than she bargained for when she invites a stranger into her home.

_____

_____

_____

_____

_____

_____

_____

_____

_____

_____

_____

_____

_____

_____

_____

_____

_____

_____

_____

_____

_____

_____

_____

_____

_____

_____

_____

_____

_____

_____

_____

_____

_____

193)   No way out. The doors are locked and Linda has no means of escape.

_____
_____
_____
_____
_____
_____
_____
_____
_____
_____
_____
_____
_____
_____
_____
_____
_____
_____
_____
_____
_____
_____
_____
_____
_____
_____
_____
_____
_____
_____
_____
_____
_____
_____

194)   There were no right answers any more. Only James knew the secret that would help them to move onto the future.

_____

_____

_____

_____

_____

_____

_____

_____

_____

_____

_____

_____

_____

_____

_____

_____

_____

_____

_____

_____

_____

_____

_____

_____

_____

_____

_____

_____

_____

_____

195)   The body was found at the foot of the cliff. Foul play was suspected.

_____

_____

_____

_____

_____

_____

_____

_____

_____

_____

_____

_____

_____

_____

_____

_____

_____

_____

_____

_____

_____

_____

_____

_____

_____

_____

_____

_____

_____

196) The door to the cellar hid secrets that Henry was too afraid to confront.

_____
_____
_____
_____
_____
_____
_____
_____
_____
_____
_____
_____
_____
_____
_____
_____
_____
_____
_____
_____
_____
_____
_____
_____
_____
_____
_____
_____
_____

197)   There had been no warning. No one suspected - not even Harry - as she lifted the shovel that was to snub out the future with one blow.

_____
_____
_____
_____
_____
_____
_____
_____
_____
_____
_____
_____
_____
_____
_____
_____
_____
_____
_____
_____
_____
_____
_____
_____
_____
_____
_____
_____
_____
_____
_____
_____
_____
_____
_____
_____
_____
_____

198) The body was found at the bottom of the cliff, but no one knows the identity of the deceased.

_____

_____

_____

_____

_____

_____

_____

_____

_____

_____

_____

_____

_____

_____

_____

_____

_____

_____

_____

_____

_____

_____

_____

_____

_____

_____

_____

_____

_____

_____

_____

199) The letter was addressed to her but sent four years ago. The difference it made to her life is crucial to her wellbeing.

_____

_____

_____

_____

_____

_____

_____

_____

_____

_____

_____

_____

_____

_____

_____

_____

_____

_____

_____

_____

_____

_____

_____

_____

_____

_____

_____

_____

_____

_____

_____

_____

200) There was no warning. When it happened, Kyle was ready to use the opportunity to get what he rightfully deserved.

_____

_____

_____

_____

_____

_____

_____

_____

_____

_____

_____

_____

_____

_____

_____

_____

_____

_____

_____

_____

_____

_____

_____

_____

_____

_____

_____

_____

_____

_____

_____

201)   As the bells struck midnight, no one knew what was happening at No. 49

202)   The initial R was all that Steven had to go on in this murder case, but it was enough to send chills down his spine.

_____

_____

_____

_____

_____

_____

_____

_____

_____

_____

_____

_____

_____

_____

_____

_____

_____

_____

_____

_____

_____

_____

_____

_____

_____

_____

_____

_____

_____

_____

_____

203)   The bottle contained poison, though the wrong person seems to have drunk it.

_____

_____

_____

_____

_____

_____

_____

_____

_____

_____

_____

_____

_____

_____

_____

_____

_____

_____

_____

_____

_____

_____

_____

_____

_____

_____

_____

_____

_____

_____

_____

_____

_____

_____

204) Where was the safe and why did father have one? When Eleanor discovers its secrets, she also understands its powers.

_____

_____

_____

_____

_____

_____

_____

_____

_____

_____

_____

_____

_____

_____

_____

_____

_____

_____

_____

_____

_____

_____

_____

_____

_____

_____

_____

_____

_____

205) The pathway at the end of the mansion garden led to a secret place where Jennifer was able to step onto the threshold of her future.

_____
_____
_____
_____
_____
_____
_____
_____
_____
_____
_____
_____
_____
_____
_____
_____
_____
_____
_____
_____
_____
_____
_____
_____
_____
_____
_____
_____
_____
_____
_____
_____
_____
_____
_____
_____
_____
_____
_____

206) Bringing the lamp from the back porch, the porch is plunged into darkness that only the eyes of Lenny could penetrate.

_____

_____

_____

_____

_____

_____

_____

_____

_____

_____

_____

_____

_____

_____

_____

_____

_____

_____

_____

_____

_____

_____

_____

_____

_____

_____

_____

_____

_____

_____

_____

207) He held the treasure chest in his hand and as she grabbed it, it tumbled down the hill toward the shore. What was in it and who would save it?

_____

_____

_____

_____

_____

_____

_____

_____

_____

_____

_____

_____

_____

_____

_____

_____

_____

_____

_____

_____

_____

_____

_____

_____

_____

_____

_____

_____

_____

_____

_____

_____

_____

_____

_____

Chapter Seventeen – Hope

In this chapter, we delve into the land of hope. The message of these stories must be clearly positive.

208)   Stuck on the island with no means of escape, Patricia saw the answer to their problem.

_____

_____

_____

_____

_____

_____

_____

_____

_____

_____

_____

_____

_____

_____

_____

_____

_____

_____

_____

_____

_____

_____

_____

_____

_____

_____

_____

_____

_____

_____

_____

_____

_____

_____

_____

209) Against the backdrop of struggle, Effie fights her way toward a new life.

_____
_____
_____
_____
_____
_____
_____
_____
_____
_____
_____
_____
_____
_____
_____
_____
_____
_____
_____
_____
_____
_____
_____
_____
_____
_____
_____
_____
_____
_____
_____
_____
_____
_____
_____
_____
_____
_____
_____

210)   Suzanne joins the nuns and as she takes her vows, feels a message from God entering into her mind.

211)   As a soldier lies on the field of battle, he sees something in the sky above him and knows he will be saved.

212)   Mike doesn't want to believe, but when Sue shows him her belief in Buddhism, he cannot escape the hope it offers him.

_____
_____
_____
_____
_____
_____
_____
_____
_____
_____
_____
_____
_____
_____
_____
_____
_____
_____
_____
_____
_____
_____
_____
_____
_____
_____
_____
_____
_____
_____
_____
_____
_____
_____
_____

213) A missionary is trapped in a village being rampaged, but one of the natives can change the course of her life.

_____

_____

_____

_____

_____

_____

_____

_____

_____

_____

_____

_____

_____

_____

_____

_____

_____

_____

_____

_____

_____

_____

_____

_____

_____

_____

_____

_____

_____

_____

_____

_____

_____

_____

_____

_____

_____

214) Grandma holds a chicken bone in her hand and makes a wish that changes the dynamics of the family to one of hope.

_____
_____
_____
_____
_____
_____
_____
_____
_____
_____
_____
_____
_____
_____
_____
_____
_____
_____
_____
_____
_____
_____
_____
_____
_____
_____
_____
_____
_____
_____
_____
_____

215)   Bernard lives in war-torn Germany though sees a sign of hope in nature that helps him to survive.

216)   Robin has no friends until he discovers that friends don't really need to be searched out. They come to you when you stop searching.

_____
_____
_____
_____
_____
_____
_____
_____
_____
_____
_____
_____
_____
_____
_____
_____
_____
_____
_____
_____
_____
_____
_____
_____
_____
_____
_____
_____
_____
_____
_____

217)   Mom has six children, not enough money for the mortgage, but she inspires hope and it pays off.

_____
_____
_____
_____
_____
_____
_____
_____
_____
_____
_____
_____
_____
_____
_____
_____
_____
_____
_____
_____
_____
_____
_____
_____
_____
_____
_____
_____
_____
_____
_____
_____
_____
_____

218) Placing the fairy at the top of the family Christmas tree gives the family new direction.

Chapter Eighteen - Sports

219) Kenny is the best basketball player on the block until his girlfriend surprises him.

_____
_____
_____
_____
_____
_____
_____
_____
_____
_____
_____
_____
_____

220) Anne likes tennis and trains to be a star. However, she falls for her coach and that spells an end to her dreams.

_____
_____
_____
_____
_____
_____
_____
_____
_____
_____
_____
_____
_____

221)   It's football on TV tonight and Sara finds a way to get her own back.

_____

_____

_____

_____

_____

_____

_____

_____

_____

_____

_____

_____

_____

_____

_____

_____

222)   Molly hates the gym and is overweight, though finds a creative solution in dancing.

_____

_____

_____

_____

_____

_____

_____

_____

_____

_____

_____

_____

_____

_____

223) Jim uses golf practice as an excuse to see his mistress, until his wife finds out the truth.

_____

_____

_____

_____

_____

_____

_____

_____

_____

_____

_____

_____

_____

_____

_____

_____

224) David needs to impress his boss with his golf skills, though falls short on the golf course. Will his character win the day?

_____

_____

_____

_____

_____

_____

_____

_____

_____

_____

_____

_____

_____

_____

_____

225) Henry can't understand his son's obsession with swimming until he meets his son's coach!

_____
_____
_____
_____
_____
_____
_____
_____
_____
_____
_____
_____
_____
_____
_____

226) In the gym, Gary shows off his muscles to the ladies, but something unexpected happens.

_____
_____
_____
_____
_____
_____
_____
_____
_____
_____
_____
_____
_____

Chapter Nineteen – Westerns

227)   Lianne wants to take over her father's farm, but does she have the stomach for it?

_____
_____
_____
_____
_____
_____
_____
_____
_____
_____
_____
_____
_____
_____
_____
_____
_____
_____
_____
_____
_____
_____
_____
_____
_____
_____
_____
_____
_____
_____
_____
_____
_____
_____

228)   Crispin doesn't like what he sees when his sister starts courting Jed. His actions change the course of their destiny.

_____
_____
_____
_____
_____
_____
_____
_____
_____
_____
_____
_____
_____
_____
_____
_____
_____
_____
_____
_____
_____
_____
_____
_____
_____
_____
_____
_____
_____
_____
_____
_____

229)   Riding horses through the countryside, Kendell finds that the Indians are more hostile than he thought.

_____
_____
_____
_____
_____
_____
_____
_____
_____
_____
_____
_____
_____
_____
_____
_____
_____
_____
_____
_____
_____
_____
_____
_____
_____
_____
_____
_____
_____
_____
_____
_____
_____
_____
_____

230) Maggie, born to a cowboy family, but brought up by the Indians, finds her peace of mind and chooses her own future.

_____
_____
_____
_____
_____
_____
_____
_____
_____
_____
_____
_____
_____
_____
_____
_____
_____
_____
_____
_____
_____
_____
_____
_____
_____
_____
_____
_____
_____
_____
_____
_____

231)   Hard hitting Kelly has to prove herself against the gunslinger coming to town to take the local sheriff hostage.

232)   Helping the apache settle into their new reservation, Charles feels that it's wrong. Can he save their burial grounds?

_____

_____

_____

_____

_____

_____

_____

_____

_____

_____

_____

_____

_____

_____

_____

_____

_____

_____

_____

_____

_____

_____

_____

_____

_____

_____

_____

_____

_____

_____

_____

_____

233) Milly joins the town women to try and drive the brothel girls out of town.

_____
_____
_____
_____
_____
_____
_____
_____
_____
_____
_____
_____
_____
_____
_____
_____
_____
_____
_____
_____
_____
_____
_____
_____
_____
_____
_____
_____
_____
_____
_____
_____
_____
_____
_____
_____
_____

234)   The Bingle Brothers are coming to town but can the town take them on and win freedom from their threat?

235) The most unlikely sheriff is appointed because of his bravery. Who is he and what made the townspeople appoint him.

_____

_____

_____

_____

_____

_____

_____

_____

_____

_____

_____

_____

_____

_____

_____

_____

_____

_____

_____

_____

_____

_____

_____

_____

_____

_____

_____

_____

_____

_____

_____

_____

_____

_____

_____

_____

236) Elliott Williams escapes jail, but before doing so, wins the heart of the Preacher's wife.

_____

_____

_____

_____

_____

_____

_____

_____

_____

_____

_____

_____

_____

_____

_____

_____

_____

_____

_____

_____

_____

_____

_____

_____

_____

_____

_____

_____

_____

_____

_____

_____

_____

_____

_____

_____

Chapter Twenty – Travel

These stories will involve travel and you can use your imagination to come up with authentic locations which will help you to improve your travel writing.

237)   Andrew travels to Thailand but little does he know what awaits him there.

_____
_____
_____
_____
_____
_____
_____
_____
_____
_____
_____

238)   Lily meets the man of her dreams in the airport, but she needs to change her airline ticket to follow her destiny.

_____
_____
_____
_____
_____
_____
_____
_____
_____
_____

239) The captain on the cruise ship is giving a dinner tonight for VIP guests, though Imogen goes missing. Will they find her?

_____
_____
_____
_____
_____
_____
_____
_____
_____
_____
_____
_____
_____
_____
_____
_____

240) Elaine restores her faith in life after visiting an ashram in Tibet.

_____
_____
_____
_____
_____
_____
_____
_____
_____
_____
_____
_____
_____
_____
_____

241) Hitchhiking across the countryside in France, Elly gets lost and her road takes her to a place that enchants her.

_____
_____
_____
_____
_____
_____
_____
_____
_____
_____
_____
_____
_____
_____
_____
_____

242) There is magic afoot when Carl discovers the magical effect that the Tuscany countryside has on his ambitions.

_____
_____
_____
_____
_____
_____
_____
_____
_____
_____
_____
_____
_____
_____
_____
_____

243) Janet and William visit Portugal and the vacation brings their marriage to a halt.

_____
_____
_____
_____
_____
_____
_____
_____
_____
_____
_____
_____
_____
_____

244) Sun, sea and sunshine, as Claire finds herself embroiled in a den of lies.

_____
_____
_____
_____
_____
_____
_____
_____
_____
_____
_____
_____
_____
_____

245) He never knew her name, but her body was amazingly beautiful.

_____
_____
_____
_____
_____
_____
_____
_____
_____
_____
_____
_____
_____
_____
_____

246) Henry travelled to the Far East to try and catch up with her, though he was too late.

_____
_____
_____
_____
_____
_____
_____
_____
_____
_____
_____
_____
_____
_____
_____

247)   James stood on the deck of the ship, knowing this farewell was a final one, as he made his way toward his new life.

_____
_____
_____
_____
_____
_____
_____
_____
_____
_____
_____
_____
_____

248)   Traveling over the sandbanks of Western Australia, Lily has to come to terms with her sexuality and her attraction toward Eleanor.

_____
_____
_____
_____
_____
_____
_____
_____
_____
_____
_____
_____
_____

Chapter Twenty One – Action and Adventure

In these stories, try to keep readers guessing. A good action and adventure story keeps the reader turning the pages.

249)   The sailboats make their way through rough waters toward a land never discovered before now. What awaits them?

_____
_____
_____
_____
_____
_____
_____
_____
_____
_____
_____
_____
_____
_____
_____
_____
_____
_____
_____
_____
_____
_____
_____
_____
_____
_____
_____
_____
_____

250) Stolen identity, but will it be any better than the old identity?

_____
_____
_____
_____
_____
_____
_____
_____
_____
_____
_____
_____
_____
_____
_____
_____
_____
_____
_____
_____
_____
_____
_____
_____
_____
_____
_____
_____
_____
_____
_____
_____
_____

251) Robbing the store at the end of the street, Perry thinks he is a millionaire! However, there's something he doesn't know.

_____

_____

_____

_____

_____

_____

_____

_____

_____

_____

_____

_____

_____

_____

_____

_____

_____

_____

_____

_____

_____

_____

_____

_____

_____

_____

_____

_____

_____

_____

_____

_____

_____

_____

_____

_____

_____

_____

_____

252) Going to church each week makes Molly look innocent, though she hides a bitter secret.

_____

_____

_____

_____

_____

_____

_____

_____

_____

_____

_____

_____

_____

_____

_____

_____

_____

_____

_____

_____

_____

_____

_____

_____

_____

_____

_____

_____

_____

_____

_____

_____

_____

_____

_____

253) The house on the end of Kerr Drive holds a terrible secret.

254) Guns and knives, Paulo's gang is encircled by law enforcement officers.

_____

_____

_____

_____

_____

_____

_____

_____

_____

_____

_____

_____

_____

_____

_____

_____

_____

_____

_____

_____

_____

_____

_____

_____

_____

_____

_____

_____

_____

255) The jewel heist – Diamonds and pearls, can they buy them happiness?

_____
_____
_____
_____
_____
_____
_____
_____
_____
_____
_____
_____
_____
_____
_____
_____
_____
_____
_____
_____
_____
_____
_____
_____
_____
_____
_____
_____
_____
_____
_____
_____

256) The car chase takes Bailey into the night away from home, though who is chasing him and why?

_____

_____

_____

_____

_____

_____

_____

_____

_____

_____

_____

_____

_____

_____

_____

_____

_____

_____

_____

_____

_____

_____

_____

_____

_____

_____

_____

_____

_____

_____

257) The bank robbery that goes wrong. Who decided upon the details and what price will he pay for his failure?

_____
_____
_____
_____
_____
_____
_____
_____
_____
_____
_____
_____
_____
_____
_____
_____
_____
_____
_____
_____
_____
_____
_____
_____
_____
_____
_____
_____
_____
_____
_____
_____
_____
_____
_____
_____
_____
_____
_____
_____
_____

258) The killer stands over the body and only when he turns it over, does he discover his mistake.

259)   The map shows the place where the treasure can be found. One part is missing. Will Larry ever find it?

_____
_____
_____
_____
_____
_____
_____
_____
_____
_____
_____
_____
_____
_____
_____
_____
_____
_____
_____
_____
_____
_____
_____
_____
_____
_____
_____
_____
_____
_____
_____
_____
_____

260)   What lies buried in Ivor's tomb? The casket is empty, but there are clues.

_____

_____

_____

_____

_____

_____

_____

_____

_____

_____

_____

_____

_____

_____

_____

_____

_____

_____

_____

_____

_____

_____

_____

_____

_____

_____

_____

_____

_____

_____

_____

_____

_____

_____

_____

261) Will Perry escape the man who has been following him? Or discover why?

262)   Harriet knows that he is being unfaithful. Angered and ready to kill, she makes her move.

263) The dark alleys of the city where prostitutes lurk makes the backdr

264)   There is no stopping Matt now that he knows who killed his father. Though does he know why?

265) The hunting party hit the forest, though Hal doesn't know one gun waits for opportunity to end his life.

Chapter Twenty Two – A twist in the Tale

266)   Hattie is tired of being ignored and decides to leave her husband. However, fate plays a cruel hand.

_____
_____
_____
_____
_____
_____
_____
_____
_____
_____
_____
_____
_____
_____
_____
_____
_____
_____
_____
_____
_____
_____
_____
_____
_____
_____
_____
_____
_____
_____

267) When two brothers come up against each other, who wins? The weak brother or the strong one?

_____

_____

_____

_____

_____

_____

_____

_____

_____

_____

_____

_____

_____

_____

_____

_____

_____

_____

_____

_____

_____

_____

_____

_____

_____

_____

_____

_____

_____

_____

_____

_____

_____

_____

_____

_____

_____

_____

_____

268)   The wishing well holds a secret. Kelly discovers quite by accident.

_____
_____
_____
_____
_____
_____
_____
_____
_____
_____
_____
_____
_____
_____
_____
_____
_____
_____
_____
_____
_____
_____
_____
_____
_____
_____
_____
_____
_____
_____
_____
_____
_____
_____
_____

269) There's no chance for Margarita to back down, now she has made her decision, but is it the right one?

_____
_____
_____
_____
_____
_____
_____
_____
_____
_____
_____
_____
_____
_____
_____
_____
_____
_____
_____
_____
_____
_____
_____
_____
_____
_____
_____
_____
_____
_____
_____
_____
_____
_____
_____
_____
_____

270) When the store is robbed and the shopkeeper killed, the police assume they have the killer.

271) The credit card fraud steals the identity of someone but a twist of fate means it has done them a favor.

_____

_____

_____

_____

_____

_____

_____

_____

_____

_____

_____

_____

_____

_____

_____

_____

_____

_____

_____

_____

_____

_____

_____

_____

_____

_____

_____

_____

_____

_____

_____

_____

_____

272) When Betty and Dave go camping in the woods, they get more than they bargained for.

273) Two women – one man, but how will Paula get him to fall for her?

_____
_____
_____
_____
_____
_____
_____
_____
_____
_____
_____
_____
_____
_____
_____
_____
_____
_____
_____
_____
_____
_____
_____
_____
_____
_____
_____
_____
_____
_____
_____
_____
_____
_____
_____

274) An envelope, long awaited, arrives, but will it give the expected result?

_____
_____
_____
_____
_____
_____
_____
_____
_____
_____
_____
_____
_____
_____
_____
_____
_____
_____
_____
_____
_____
_____
_____
_____
_____
_____
_____
_____
_____
_____
_____

275) Sara is happy with her life until she loses everything. How will she get back to her state of happiness?

_____

_____

_____

_____

_____

_____

_____

_____

_____

_____

_____

_____

_____

_____

_____

_____

_____

_____

_____

_____

_____

_____

_____

_____

_____

_____

_____

_____

_____

_____

_____

_____

_____

_____

276) There are four brothers but only one can inherit the house. Why does it go to Jonathan?

_____

_____

_____

_____

_____

_____

_____

_____

_____

_____

_____

_____

_____

_____

_____

_____

_____

_____

_____

_____

_____

_____

_____

_____

_____

_____

_____

_____

_____

_____

_____

277) Nicole wants to be a nurse but quickly changes her mind when something in her life changes.

278) There are no prizes for being the best, although John outdoes all expectations.

_____

_____

_____

_____

_____

_____

_____

_____

_____

_____

_____

_____

_____

_____

_____

_____

_____

_____

_____

_____

_____

_____

_____

_____

_____

_____

_____

_____

_____

279) Opening the door to the closed barn, shock awaits Janine, but will she ever be able to move on?

_____

_____

_____

_____

_____

_____

_____

_____

_____

_____

_____

_____

_____

_____

_____

_____

_____

_____

_____

_____

_____

_____

_____

_____

_____

_____

_____

_____

_____

_____

_____

_____

_____

_____

_____

_____

_____

Chapter Twenty Three – Memoirs

This chapter gives you a good chance to use and hone first person narrative. Pretend you are the heroine or hero of the story and see it from your perspective.

280) The hiding place – somewhere safe and somewhere secure but not always.

_____
_____
_____
_____
_____
_____
_____
_____
_____
_____
_____
_____
_____
_____
_____
_____
_____
_____
_____
_____
_____
_____
_____
_____
_____

281) A dream brings about a solution, but how can Kathy persuade her husband?

_____
_____
_____
_____
_____
_____
_____
_____
_____
_____
_____
_____
_____
_____
_____
_____
_____
_____
_____
_____
_____
_____
_____
_____
_____
_____
_____
_____
_____
_____
_____

282)   The town is filled with gossip but can Kelly evade the gossipers

_____
_____
_____
_____
_____
_____
_____
_____
_____
_____
_____
_____
_____
_____
_____
_____
_____
_____
_____
_____
_____
_____
_____
_____
_____
_____
_____
_____
_____
_____
_____
_____
_____

283) There are no words to describe the coldness of his heart.

284)   Opening a letter changes Molly's life forever. Is that good?

_____
_____
_____
_____
_____
_____
_____
_____
_____
_____
_____
_____
_____
_____
_____
_____
_____
_____
_____
_____
_____
_____
_____
_____
_____
_____
_____
_____
_____
_____
_____

285) Childhood memories turn into today's reality.

_____
_____
_____
_____
_____
_____
_____
_____
_____
_____
_____
_____
_____
_____
_____
_____
_____
_____
_____
_____
_____
_____
_____
_____
_____
_____
_____
_____
_____
_____
_____
_____
_____

286) The elder sister was always the preferred one until things drastically changed.

_____
_____
_____
_____
_____
_____
_____
_____
_____
_____
_____
_____
_____
_____
_____
_____
_____
_____
_____
_____
_____
_____
_____
_____
_____
_____
_____
_____
_____

287) A car accident leaves Harriet crippled for life, but she is a survivor.

_____
_____
_____
_____
_____
_____
_____
_____
_____
_____
_____
_____
_____
_____
_____
_____
_____
_____
_____
_____
_____
_____
_____
_____
_____
_____
_____
_____
_____
_____
_____
_____
_____
_____

288) Henry reflects over his life and is filled with regret.

_____
_____
_____
_____
_____
_____
_____
_____
_____
_____
_____
_____
_____
_____
_____
_____
_____
_____
_____
_____
_____
_____
_____
_____
_____
_____
_____
_____
_____
_____
_____

289) Millicent knows that if she doesn't apologize, there's no going back. Will she?

290) Finding out from a stranger that you have been betrayed, but how do you react?

_____
_____
_____
_____
_____
_____
_____
_____
_____
_____
_____
_____
_____
_____
_____
_____
_____
_____
_____
_____
_____
_____
_____
_____
_____
_____
_____
_____
_____
_____
_____
_____
_____

291) The affair with the stranger. Strangers no more.

_____
_____
_____
_____
_____
_____
_____
_____
_____
_____
_____
_____
_____
_____
_____
_____
_____
_____
_____
_____
_____
_____
_____
_____
_____
_____
_____
_____
_____
_____

292) Waiting for the right moment, our heroine finds the right time to make drastic changes in her life.

293) That first journey into a foreign country brings surprises and suspense.

_____
_____
_____
_____
_____
_____
_____
_____
_____
_____
_____
_____
_____
_____
_____
_____
_____
_____
_____
_____
_____
_____
_____
_____
_____
_____
_____
_____
_____
_____
_____
_____
_____
_____

294)   Working behind the scenes in a hospital, Kirsty has to face up to the death of a child patient.

295) Told from the point of view of the patient, this story recounts the history of an old lady about to die.

_____

_____

_____

_____

_____

_____

_____

_____

_____

_____

_____

_____

_____

_____

_____

_____

_____

_____

_____

_____

_____

_____

_____

_____

_____

_____

_____

_____

_____

_____

_____

_____

_____

_____

_____

_____

_____

_____

_____

_____

Chapter Twenty Four – Words and sounds

This time, try to use words throughout the story which rhyme with the word given. Be imaginative and do use your dictionary to widen your vocabulary.

296)   The story can be about anything, but words used within the story must include words that sound like "please."

_____
_____
_____
_____
_____
_____
_____
_____
_____
_____
_____
_____
_____
_____
_____
_____
_____
_____
_____
_____
_____
_____
_____
_____
_____
_____

297)   Since the hero of the story is Jim, you must include words that sound like his name.

_____
_____
_____
_____
_____
_____
_____
_____
_____
_____
_____
_____
_____
_____
_____
_____
_____
_____
_____
_____
_____
_____
_____
_____
_____
_____
_____
_____
_____
_____
_____
_____
_____
_____
_____

298)   In this story about two brothers, use words that sound like TWO

_____
_____
_____
_____
_____
_____
_____
_____
_____
_____
_____
_____
_____
_____
_____
_____
_____
_____
_____
_____
_____
_____
_____
_____
_____
_____
_____
_____
_____
_____
_____
_____
_____
_____
_____
_____
_____
_____

299) Words that sound like grave should be used in this story about a young woman seeking her destiny.

_____

_____

_____

_____

_____

_____

_____

_____

_____

_____

_____

_____

_____

_____

_____

_____

_____

_____

_____

_____

_____

_____

_____

_____

_____

_____

_____

_____

_____

_____

_____

_____

_____

_____

_____

_____

_____

300) In this story of a workman trying to earn enough to go abroad, the word you need to rhyme with is pleasure.

301) The sound of the word is treasure. It is the story of a young man seeking to lose his virginity.

_____
_____
_____
_____
_____
_____
_____
_____
_____
_____
_____
_____
_____
_____
_____
_____
_____
_____
_____
_____
_____
_____
_____
_____
_____
_____
_____
_____
_____
_____
_____
_____
_____
_____
_____
_____

302)   In this story try to use words that sound like "yet" including two two-syllable words.

_____

_____

_____

_____

_____

_____

_____

_____

_____

_____

_____

_____

_____

_____

_____

_____

_____

_____

_____

_____

_____

_____

_____

_____

_____

_____

_____

_____

_____

_____

_____

_____

_____

303) Can Janine find her cat? In this story, use descriptions that suggest the sound of the lost kitten.

_____
_____
_____
_____
_____
_____
_____
_____
_____
_____
_____
_____
_____
_____
_____
_____
_____
_____
_____
_____
_____
_____
_____
_____
_____
_____
_____
_____
_____
_____
_____
_____
_____
_____

304) Harriet has to tell the children their father is dead. Use words that sound like grief.

305) In this story, use your imagination to incorporate words that sound like "Bring"

Chapter Twenty-Five – Video Games

There are many popular computer games, but you need to imagine your own. Base your stories on imaginative games that will be fun for adults.

306) When Marvin tries to beat his brother at a video game, his brother pulls out all the stops to win.

_____

_____

_____

_____

_____

_____

_____

_____

_____

_____

_____

_____

_____

_____

_____

_____

_____

_____

_____

_____

_____

_____

_____

_____

_____

_____

_____

307) It's a war game and Jimmy needs to make sure his guns have enough ammunition to beat the enemy. Will he survive?

_____
_____
_____
_____
_____
_____
_____
_____
_____
_____
_____
_____
_____
_____
_____
_____
_____
_____
_____
_____
_____
_____
_____
_____
_____
_____
_____
_____
_____
_____
_____
_____
_____

308) Flight path is set for the space shuttle, but something goes wrong.

309) Harriet has to remember which card is which in this game but cheats. How?

310) Shooting all the baddies gets tough when Max discovers they shoot back!

311)   Carlos gets lost in a video game battle with a stranger, who turns out to be very attractive.

_____
_____
_____
_____
_____
_____
_____
_____
_____
_____
_____
_____
_____
_____
_____
_____
_____
_____
_____
_____
_____
_____
_____
_____
_____
_____
_____
_____
_____
_____
_____
_____
_____
_____
_____
_____

312)   It started as a harmless game, but turned into a deadly pursuit.

_____
_____
_____
_____
_____
_____
_____
_____
_____
_____
_____
_____
_____
_____
_____
_____
_____
_____
_____
_____
_____
_____
_____
_____
_____
_____
_____
_____
_____

313) Video game characters turn into real characters and the result is murder.

Chapter Twenty Six – Birthday Parties

Let your imagination soar and imagine parties that are fun and laughter for everyone!

314) Patty is embarrassed when she finds Dave has invited one of her old flames to her birthday party.

_____

_____

_____

_____

_____

_____

_____

_____

_____

_____

_____

_____

_____

_____

_____

_____

_____

_____

_____

_____

_____

_____

_____

_____

315)   George suggests an outing for Beverley's birthday, but when she finds out where, she hits the roof!

_____
_____
_____
_____
_____
_____
_____
_____
_____
_____
_____
_____
_____
_____
_____
_____
_____
_____
_____
_____
_____
_____
_____
_____
_____
_____
_____
_____
_____
_____
_____
_____
_____

316) The relationship between mother and daughter – the birthday conundrum

317) Alex is determined that Sue will get the best surprise ever for her birthday but is it something she wants?

_____
_____
_____
_____
_____
_____
_____
_____
_____
_____
_____
_____
_____
_____
_____
_____
_____
_____
_____
_____
_____
_____
_____
_____
_____
_____
_____
_____
_____
_____
_____
_____
_____

318) Kerry gets reminded of the passing of time when faced with too many candles and being confronted by reality.

_____
_____
_____
_____
_____
_____
_____
_____
_____
_____
_____
_____
_____
_____
_____
_____
_____
_____
_____
_____
_____
_____
_____
_____
_____
_____
_____
_____
_____
_____
_____
_____

319)   The birthday party ends in tears when Elaine's mother decides to spill a few home truths.

320) The birthday party planned for Kara's father goes horribly wrong.

_____
_____
_____
_____
_____
_____
_____
_____
_____
_____
_____
_____
_____
_____
_____
_____
_____
_____
_____
_____
_____
_____
_____
_____
_____
_____
_____
_____
_____
_____
_____
_____
_____
_____
_____

321)   A party, a gathering of friends who soon become enemies.

_____

_____

_____

_____

_____

_____

_____

_____

_____

_____

_____

_____

_____

_____

_____

_____

_____

_____

_____

_____

_____

_____

_____

_____

_____

_____

_____

_____

_____

_____

_____

_____

_____

_____

322) When Jimmy is asked what he wants for his birthday, his answer changes his life forever.

_____
_____
_____
_____
_____
_____
_____
_____
_____
_____
_____
_____
_____
_____
_____
_____
_____
_____
_____
_____
_____
_____
_____
_____
_____
_____
_____
_____
_____
_____
_____
_____

323) There is no escaping age. Flora looks back on her life while celebrating her 90th birthday.

324) The ghost of Paul visits his wife to give her the best gift ever.

325) Birthdays spent alone push Stewart off the edge. Who will rescue him?

_____
_____
_____
_____
_____
_____
_____
_____
_____
_____
_____
_____
_____
_____
_____
_____
_____
_____
_____
_____
_____
_____
_____
_____
_____
_____
_____
_____
_____
_____
_____

326) It's time to celebrate, but it's not so much the birthday, but the beginning of something new.

_____
_____
_____
_____
_____
_____
_____
_____
_____
_____
_____
_____
_____
_____
_____
_____
_____
_____
_____
_____
_____
_____
_____
_____
_____
_____
_____

327) A birthday to remember. Jean looks back with affection, though bitterness gets in the way of happiness.

328) She dreamed of an engagement ring. However, that wasn't what she got.

329) It's hard getting old. It's harder when you know your husband's mistress is 20 years younger than you are.

_____
_____
_____
_____
_____
_____
_____
_____
_____
_____
_____
_____
_____
_____
_____
_____
_____
_____
_____
_____
_____
_____
_____
_____
_____
_____
_____
_____
_____
_____
_____
_____
_____
_____
_____
_____
_____

330) When teen twins are trusted with the home on their birthday, bad things happen.

331) When Jamie finds out his wife is unfaithful, he uses her allergy as a means to get rid of her.

332) Elizabeth celebrates her 30th birthday in hospital with cancer. However, good news awaits her.

_____
_____
_____
_____
_____
_____
_____
_____
_____
_____
_____
_____
_____
_____
_____
_____
_____
_____
_____
_____
_____
_____
_____
_____
_____
_____
_____
_____
_____

333)   The bracelet Jackie saw in her husband's pocket wasn't intended for her. How does she find out?

_____
_____
_____
_____
_____
_____
_____
_____
_____
_____
_____
_____
_____
_____
_____
_____
_____
_____
_____
_____
_____
_____
_____
_____
_____
_____
_____
_____
_____
_____
_____
_____
_____
_____
_____
_____

334) Barry wants to get married on his birthday, but Hilary has other ideas.

_____
_____
_____
_____
_____
_____
_____
_____
_____
_____
_____
_____
_____
_____
_____
_____
_____
_____
_____
_____
_____
_____
_____
_____
_____
_____
_____
_____
_____
_____
_____

335) The church bell strikes midnight and Kathleen comes of age and is accepted as the wife of a werewolf.

336) It's going to be hard for Wanda to enjoy her birthday party in a wheelchair, especially when it was her husband who put her there.

_____
_____
_____
_____
_____
_____
_____
_____
_____
_____
_____
_____
_____
_____
_____
_____
_____
_____
_____
_____
_____
_____
_____
_____
_____
_____
_____
_____
_____
_____
_____
_____
_____
_____

337) Clara wants a horse for her birthday, though mom thinks differently!

_____
_____
_____
_____
_____
_____
_____
_____
_____
_____
_____
_____
_____
_____
_____
_____
_____
_____
_____
_____
_____
_____
_____
_____
_____
_____
_____
_____
_____
_____
_____

338) Philip fell over and knocked over the birthday cake!

Chapter Twenty Seven – Seasons

In this chapter, you need to think about descriptions. If you were to describe a winter's day, you need to use words that give you a picture in your mind of cold weather, snow and ice. If you choose summer, similarly you would make someone think of heat.

339)   Spring is happening and love is in the air as Emile and Lottie fall in love in Paris.

_____
_____
_____
_____
_____
_____
_____
_____
_____
_____
_____
_____
_____
_____
_____
_____
_____
_____
_____
_____
_____
_____
_____
_____
_____
_____
_____

340) The winter chill hangs over the graveyard as one more grave is dug for someone who died before his time.

341) The cold cloak of winter gets into the bones as Millicent comes to terms with the fact that her life is over.

342) It's winter, and the lake is frozen. How does Heidi hide the body of her lover?

_____

_____

_____

_____

_____

_____

_____

_____

_____

_____

_____

_____

_____

_____

_____

_____

_____

_____

_____

_____

_____

_____

_____

_____

_____

_____

_____

_____

_____

_____

_____

_____

_____

_____

_____

343) The spring arrives and with it, all the flowers of spring. Henry looks at the new life that lies ahead with optimism.

_____
_____
_____
_____
_____
_____
_____
_____
_____
_____
_____
_____
_____
_____
_____
_____
_____
_____
_____
_____
_____
_____
_____
_____
_____
_____
_____
_____
_____
_____
_____
_____
_____

344) Sun, sand and romance, but how will Emma react when she finds Pedro has been insincere?

_____

_____

_____

_____

_____

_____

_____

_____

_____

_____

_____

_____

_____

_____

_____

_____

_____

_____

_____

_____

_____

_____

_____

_____

_____

_____

_____

_____

_____

_____

_____

_____

_____

_____

_____

345) There's no place like home after a vacation away, but the home may not be as safe as the Evans family supposed.

_____
_____
_____
_____
_____
_____
_____
_____
_____
_____
_____
_____
_____
_____
_____
_____
_____
_____
_____
_____
_____
_____
_____
_____
_____
_____
_____
_____
_____
_____
_____
_____
_____
_____
_____
_____
_____
_____
_____
_____
_____
_____

346) Summer romance, but can it bloom into the next season?

_____
_____
_____
_____
_____
_____
_____
_____
_____
_____
_____
_____
_____
_____
_____
_____
_____
_____
_____
_____
_____
_____
_____
_____
_____
_____
_____
_____
_____
_____
_____
_____
_____
_____
_____

347) Golden leaves tumbling from the trees – Lilian seeks out the treasures of nature as she reminisces about her love for her husband who has now gone.

_____
_____
_____
_____
_____
_____
_____
_____
_____
_____
_____
_____
_____
_____
_____
_____
_____
_____
_____
_____
_____
_____
_____
_____
_____
_____
_____
_____
_____
_____
_____

Chapter Twenty Eight – Character Development

One of the most important aspects of fiction writing is character development. In this section use the prompts to come up with stories about characters and make their characters come alive on the page.

348) Eleanor should be modeled upon a woman you know as she goes through a dangerous situation when held at gunpoint.

_____
_____
_____
_____
_____
_____
_____
_____
_____
_____
_____
_____
_____
_____
_____
_____
_____
_____
_____
_____
_____
_____
_____
_____

349) The Bank Manager says no to Kevin and ruins his dreams. Will he retaliate?

350) There are two sisters, but each has very individual ideas about what's right and what's wrong.

_____
_____
_____
_____
_____
_____
_____
_____
_____
_____
_____
_____
_____
_____
_____
_____
_____
_____
_____
_____
_____
_____
_____
_____
_____
_____
_____
_____
_____

351)   A man who lives on the streets finds joy in the rising sun of a summer's day.

_____
_____
_____
_____
_____
_____
_____
_____
_____
_____
_____
_____
_____
_____
_____
_____
_____
_____
_____
_____
_____
_____
_____
_____
_____
_____
_____
_____
_____
_____
_____
_____
_____
_____

352)   Jan is a bag lady. Her view of life is tainted by a past that haunts her.

353) Mrs. Hillier has never done anything wrong in her life. This time she did and the cops are after her.

354) . Robin didn't realize how much he hurt his girlfriend until she decides to take revenge.

355) The teacher was a widower, though those who knew him wondered if he had been responsible for his wife's death.

356) The perfect scholar – though was she? What was it that Heather kept hidden from those who knew her?

_____
_____
_____
_____
_____
_____
_____
_____
_____
_____
_____
_____
_____
_____
_____
_____
_____
_____
_____
_____
_____
_____
_____
_____
_____
_____
_____
_____
_____
_____
_____
_____
_____
_____
_____

357) Growing up in a mining town, Alex has a chip on his shoulder as he starts his political career.

_____
_____
_____
_____
_____
_____
_____
_____
_____
_____
_____
_____
_____
_____
_____
_____
_____
_____
_____
_____
_____
_____
_____
_____
_____
_____
_____
_____
_____
_____
_____
_____
_____
_____

358) Jennifer wasn't the smartest card in the pack, but even she knew what he did to her was wrong.

359)   Oliver looked her in the eye. What he said changed her view of him forever.

360)   There was only one inheritor. The other family members had been cut out of his will.

_____
_____
_____
_____
_____
_____
_____
_____
_____
_____
_____
_____
_____
_____
_____
_____
_____
_____
_____
_____
_____
_____
_____
_____
_____
_____
_____
_____
_____
_____

361)   Tyler didn't know how to tell his grandparents the truth. They would never have understood.

_____
_____
_____
_____
_____
_____
_____
_____
_____
_____
_____
_____
_____
_____
_____
_____
_____
_____
_____
_____
_____
_____
_____
_____
_____
_____
_____
_____
_____
_____
_____
_____
_____
_____

362) Gabriella was beautiful, but there was a side to her nature that was abhorrent.

_____

_____

_____

_____

_____

_____

_____

_____

_____

_____

_____

_____

_____

_____

_____

_____

_____

_____

_____

_____

_____

_____

_____

_____

_____

_____

_____

_____

_____

_____

363) Gregory didn't want to become a killer, but he was left with no choice.

364) Allen was brought up to believe in God, though his faith faltered, when his wife died suddenly aged 32.

365) A lone islander, suspicious of strangers, lets down his guard for Mary.

_____

_____

_____

_____

_____

_____

_____

_____

_____

_____

_____

_____

_____

_____

_____

_____

_____

_____

_____

_____

_____

_____

_____

_____

_____

_____

_____

_____

_____

_____

_____

_____

Conclusion

If you chose one story in multiple option chapters, go back and try to write the other story. You will find that you have become more fluent as a writer and the second time around may not find them as taxing. I hope that you have enjoyed this book and that you have learned all about character development, narrative, description and sounds and that you have enjoyed your journey into the land of fiction.

Sometimes when you suffer from writer's block, it's hard to find ideas and that's where this book helps you to be able to keep writing and keep finding new approaches that help you to move forward as a writer.

Leave Us a Review!

www.LeaveHonest.Review/365Prompts

Thank you for all the support!
You keep my family fed and happy!

We couldn't do it without you!

www.tmcrane.org/101kids

www.ingramcontent.com/pod-product-compliance
Lightning Source LLC
Chambersburg PA
CBHW081146280526
45787CB00008B/3240